Published by Ruff Moore Media Publishing

Title: Mommy, I Can Do It: Learning Self Care (A part of the series "Mommy, I Can Do It")

Book Cover by Kim Ruff Moore Illustrations by Kim Ruff Moore ISBN: 979-8-8693-6521-7

For permissions requests or inquiries, contact Ruff Moore Media Publishing at the addresses below:

www.kimruffmoore.com www.ruffmooremedia.com

Printed in the United States.

May each little one grow,discover,
learn and achieve

Other Titles by this Author

- "Suzzie Mocha Series"
- "Kirby the Koala Series"
- "Sergio the Studio Mouse Series"
- "Spence Seven Series"
- "Harper Sharper Series"
- "Pavo the Parrot"
- "Otis the Brave Brown Bear"
- "Rosie and the Easter Egg Hunt"
- "The Land of Unicorns Series"
- "Bria Gets New Braids For School"
- "Elo The Elephant Forgets Everything"
- "Piper The Pretty Pink Dinosaur Series"
- Kids Prayers Series
- Mommy, I Can Do It Series

Mommy, I Can Do It: Learning Self Care

by Kim Ruff Moore

In a bustling neighborhood filled with laughter and joy, there lived a group of adventurous little ones: Tiffany, Morgan, Amy, Brittany, Chloe, Piper, Regan, Summer, Journey, Aiden, Tucker, and Spencer. Each day brought new discoveries and challenges, but today was special—it was the day they would each learn something new.

Tiffany, with her curly hair bouncing, decided it was time to conquer handwashing. With determination in her eyes, she approached the sink, pumped the soap, and lathered her hands like a pro. With giggles and splashes, she rinsed off the bubbles, feeling accomplished.

Spencer, the mischievous one, was on a mission to master brushing his teeth. Armed with a colorful toothbrush and minty paste, he scrubbed away, making sure to reach every tooth. With a sparkling smile, he proudly showed off his pearly whites to anyone who would look.

Meanwhile, Amy, the quiet observer, took on the task of tidying up her toys. With a sigh and a smile, she gathered her scattered treasures and placed them neatly in their bins. As she surveyed her clean play area, she felt a sense of peace and satisfaction wash over her.

Brittany, the bubbly ball of energy, decided it was time to tackle a chore: setting the table for dinner. With plates in hand and a skip in her step, she carefully arranged them on the table, feeling like a little hostess preparing for a grand feast.

Chloe, with her bright eyes and curious nature, was determined to learn how to comb her hair. With gentle strokes, she untangled the knots and smoothed down her unruly locks, feeling more grown-up with each pass of the comb.

Piper, the fearless explorer, ventured into the kitchen to learn how to pour herself a glass of lemonade. With steady hands and a steady gaze, she filled her cup to the brim, proud of her newfound independence.

LEMONADE

Regan, the thoughtful one, decided it was time to learn how to make her bed. With precision and care, she smoothed out the sheets and fluffed the pillows, creating a cozy nest to crawl into at the end of the day.

Summer, with her sunny disposition, tackled the task of watering the plants. With a little watering can in hand, she carefully poured water onto each leaf, nurturing her green friends with love and care.

Journey, the determined dreamer, set her sights on learning how to tie her shoes. With fingers fumbling and loops twisting, she persevered until she finally mastered the art of the perfect bow, a proud smile spreading across her face.

Aiden, the playful prankster, decided it was time to learn how to wash his face all by himself. With a splash of water and a dollop of soap, he lathered up his tiny hands and gently washed away the day's adventures, his laughter mingling with the sound of water running as he transformed a simple task into a joyful ritual of self-care, his face beaming with pride at his newfound independence.

Tucker, the little helper, took on the task of organizing his clothes in the dresser. With determination in his eyes, he folded each shirt and pair of pants with care, arranging them neatly in their designated drawers. With each item in its proper place, he felt a sense of accomplishment and satisfaction, knowing that he was taking an important step towards independence and tidiness.

As the day drew to a close and the sun dipped below the horizon, each toddler tucked into bed, feeling a sense of pride and accomplishment in all they had learned and achieved. Tomorrow would bring new challenges and tasks to conquer, but they knew they were ready to face them with the same enthusiasm and determination, armed with the skills of little helpers ready to make a big difference in their world.

Epilogue:

As the sun sets on another day filled with laughter, learning, and love, we reflect on the journey of our little ones through the pages of "Mommy, I Can Do It: Learning Self Care"

In these colorful tales, Tiffany, Morgan, Amy, Brittany, Chloe, Piper, Regan, Summer, Journey, Aiden, Tucker, and Spencer discovered the joy of independence and responsibility. From brushing teeth to organizing toys, from washing hands to setting the table, each young one embarked on their own unique path towards self-discovery and growth.

Through their triumphs, both big and small, our little ones learned valuable lessons about perseverance, patience, and the importance of taking care of themselves and their surroundings. With each task mastered, they gained confidence and a sense of pride in their abilities, laying the foundation for a lifetime of success.

As parents, caregivers, and educators, we celebrate these moments of triumph with them, cherishing the memories of their first steps towards independence. And as we turn the final page of this book, we look forward to the countless adventures and discoveries that lie ahead for our little ones, knowing that they are well-equipped to face whatever challenges come their way.

May this book serve as a reminder of the incredible journey of growth and development that our little ones embark on each day, and may it inspire us all to celebrate the small victories and cherish the precious moments along the way.

Meet the Author

Kim Ruff Moore is a multifaceted artist whose talents have touched hearts across the globe. As a Stellar Award-winning singer-songwriter and national recording artist, Kim's voice carries messages of hope and inspiration. Beyond her musical achievements, Kim has established herself as a prolific author with an impressive repertoire of 45 published books. Her works span various genres, from children's literature to insightful guides on finances and relationships. Kim's dedication to uplifting others is evident in the five-star ratings her books consistently receive.

A champion of literacy, Kim has created several beloved book series for children, including "Suzzie Mocha," "Spence Seven," "Sergio the Studio Mouse," "Kirby the Koala," Kids Prayers, Mommy, I can do it, and "Harper Sharper," among others. Through imaginative storytelling, Kim instills valuable lessons and fosters creativity in young minds.

Kim's creative endeavors extend beyond the written word. She is a proud member of the duo group "The New Consolers," alongside her husband, Jeffrey Moore, who is a renowned music producer with roots in the legendary Sam Cooke band. Jeffrey's induction into the DooWap Hall of Fame in 2013 is a testament to his musical legacy.

Together, Kim and Jeffrey captivate audiences worldwide with their soul-stirring performances. Their shared passion for music and storytelling creates an unforgettable experience for listeners of all ages.

In addition to her artistic pursuits, Kim generously shares her literary platform at various functions and speaking engagements, inspiring others to pursue their passions and fulfill their potential.

Kim and Jeffrey's family life is equally enriching, with four children who undoubtedly inherit their parents' creativity and drive. Their son Spencer, also a writer, serves as the inspiration behind the acclaimed "Spence Seven" book series, continuing the family's legacy of storytelling and inspiration.

Through her music, writing, and advocacy, Kim Ruff Moore continues to make a profound impact, spreading joy and empowerment wherever her talents take her.

9 798869 365217

Printed by Libri Plureos GmbH in Hamburg,
Germany